Treat me right

A Woman's Guide to the Perfect Relationship

by D. Light

Illustrations Dina Djabieva

Calligraphy/Illustrated Letters Renée Troy

© Light the World Publishing

Printed in Hong Kong

Foreword

This book was created as a
gift of love to all those
who read it. So that
all the walls in our
hearts disappear and
bridges of respect
and tenderness take
their place.

Treat me right

Do's

Listen to me

Respect
me

Give me
the benefit
of the doubt

pologize

when you

hurt me

Give me
a
second
chance

et me
grow
and learn
in your
presence

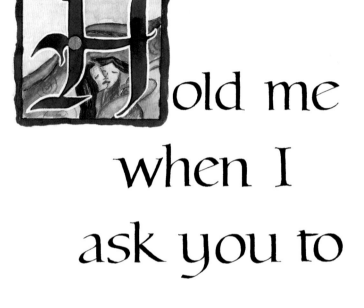old me
when I
ask you to

n a world

of strangers,

be my friend

rust me

on me

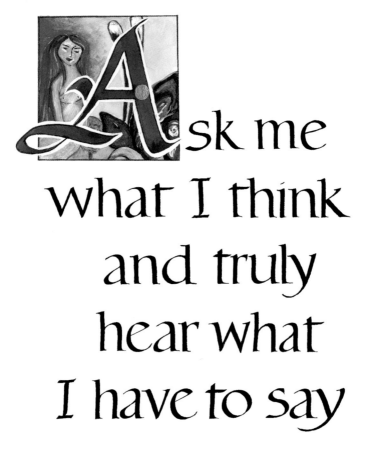

sk me
what I think
and truly
hear what
I have to say

Care
about me

Be grateful
that
I'm alive

Treat me right

Don'ts

Don't shut me out

Don't be cruel

on't forget
to say
thank you

Don't leave without saying goodbye

And if you love me and need me, don't let a day go by without letting me know

Treat me right

Maybe's

When in
doubt, ask

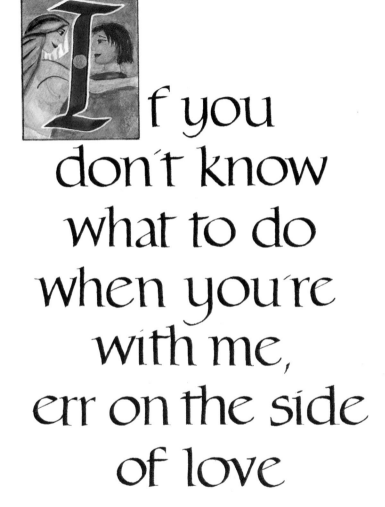

If you
don't know
what to do
when you're
with me,
err on the side
of love

Being right doesn't solve anything, maybe being compassionate does

Maybe
fear comes
from pain in
your past.
Maybe love
comes from
letting it go

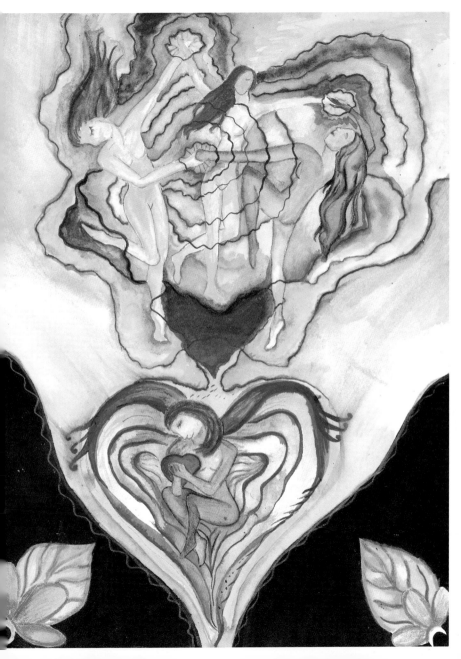

aybe

the time we
spend together
will change
our lives, so
treat me right

nd I
promise to do
all of
these things
for you too,
because
I love you so